IMAGES
of America

FORT BRAGG

On the Cover: Pictured in 1900, two ladies motor along a plank road through the redwoods, connecting the eastern terminus of the California Western Railroad between Fort Bragg and Willits. (Photograph by W.T. Fitch.)

IMAGES
of America

FORT BRAGG

Sylvia E. Bartley

ARCADIA
PUBLISHING

ISBN 978-1-4671-3085-1

Published by Arcadia Publishing
Charleston, South Carolina

Printed in the United States of America

Library of Congress Control Number: 2013939795

For all general information, please contact Arcadia Publishing:
Telephone 843-853-2070
Fax 843-853-0044
E-mail sales@arcadiapublishing.com
For customer service and orders:
Toll-Free 1-888-313-2665

Visit us on the Internet at www.arcadiapublishing.com

This pictorial is dedicated to those rare individuals who have the foresight to preserve their community's history—for the past lights a path to the future.

CONTENTS

Acknowledgments

The history of Fort Bragg, California, has been collected by a number of local residents who went to considerable trouble and expense to record parts of this complex story. Most people documented their own experience, family, and friends. The organization that finally brought many of these pieces together is the Fort Bragg–Mendocino Coast Historical Society, based in Fort Bragg, the largest town on the coast in Mendocino County.

The following local organizations deserve special recognition for their efforts to preserve Fort Bragg's history: the Fort Bragg–Mendocino Coast Historical Society, Fort Bragg; the Grace Hudson Museum, Ukiah; the Kelley House Museum, Mendocino; the Mendocino County Historical Society, Ukiah; the Mendocino County Museum, Willits; and Noyo Hill House, Fort Bragg.

We give special thanks to Rick Hemmings for sharing his unique Pomo villages and trails maps and ideas. In addition to the author's collection, others who generously shared their personal collections for this story include Ben Booth, Kevin V. Bunker, Abbie Colbert, David Foucheaux, C.J. Johnson, Wilbur J. Lawson, Harriet Rhoades, and Denise Stenberg.

Most of the photographs come from the collections in the Archives of the Fort Bragg–Mendocino Coast Historical Society (FB–MCHS), which also manages historical materials held by the City of Fort Bragg. Georgia-Pacific donated historical materials chiefly created by the Union Lumber Company (1885–1969). Local residents donated their historical photographs and documents to the Union Lumber Company's Museum, to the City of Fort Bragg, and to FB–MCHS for preservation, display, research, and study.

Thanks are due to Arcadia Publishing's editors for bearing with me through the year that the FB–MCHS Archives required to be moved and reorganized before this project could even begin. I thank Bill Mulvihill for graphics assistance and David Foucheaux for both technical support and fact-checking.

I also thank my husband, Russell, for his patience, endless encouragement, and cheerful support throughout this project.

Unless otherwise noted, all images appear courtesy of FB-MCHS.

Introduction

More than 12,000 years before white men came to stay, the coastal area now known as Fort Bragg was home to the Coast Yukis and, later, to Pomoan people who migrated to the coast from Lake County and several inland valleys in Mendocino County. The Pomos were being pushed out of their traditional living and gathering areas by the whites. Abundant resources allowed for a mostly peaceful lifestyle close to the land. Extended family groups collected seafood, salt, and kelp in the summers to last through the winter in their more sheltered inland villages, removed from the storm-lashed coast.

Traditionally, each family group "owned" rights to certain gathering areas. Outsiders asked permission for access. In times of poor acorn crops and scarce resources inland, coastal gathering areas were shared. Natives collected for their own needs and to trade for items they could not provide for themselves. The population remained at sustainable levels.

Although there were seven different Pomoan languages, they shared a culture, basic lifeways, and values. They gathered annually for a "Big Time." Villages took turns being hosts. These gatherings also brought young people together. Trade and intermarriages promoted peaceful relations. Made from native plants they collected, prepared, and sewed or wove into decorative vessels for many uses, Pomo basketry is world-famous. Besides tote and storage baskets, men wove snares and nets to catch small game or fish. The women made decorated gift baskets and cooking baskets that were watertight. Willow-framed houses covered with tule mats and tule canoes were also watertight. Babies were laced into willow-framed cradle baskets that became their chairs once the youngsters could walk.

Although most large Pomo villages were located inland, a few permanent villages existed in more protected locations near the coast, especially after outsiders came. One coastal Northern Pomo village was Kah-lah-deh-mun, meaning "surrounded by trees," in an open glade where coastal pine trees protected its inhabitants from prevailing northwest winds. The nearby rocky shore provided seafood, kelp, and salt. Away from the ocean's cold, salty winds, redwood trees grew tall, climbing the coastal hills. Their specially shaped leaves collected fog and dripped onto their feet. Streams emerged from their interlaced roots. Shady redwood groves were too cool to live beneath, but fallen branches provided firewood, and Pomos pried off thick pieces of redwood bark, using elk antlers as wedges, to construct coastal shelters. Their village site, protected from the prevailing northwest winds, would become the future Fort Bragg.

The inland climate was warmer. Oaks, buckeyes, and other trees and vegetation provided seasonal acorns, nuts, and seeds, staples of their diet, which they ground into flour for bread, mush, and soup. They gathered fresh greens and dried wild berries and herbs to flavor their food and make medicines. They hunted deer, birds, squirrels, and rabbits. Feathers decorated baskets; skins became skirts, capes, or blankets. They made bone fishing hooks and chipped points and hand axes from local rocks like chert and, in Lake County, from obsidian. Rivers flowing down from the coastal mountains teemed with salmon and trout in season. They constructed rafts and, on occasion, dugout canoes. They also made "money" out of clamshells to secure by trade what they could not supply for themselves.

Explorers had long sailed by, seeking the fabled riches of the Seven Cities of Gold. The treasure they brought back to their patrons in the Old World fueled the Industrial Revolution. By the mid-16th century whalers plied the northern coast, hunting whales for their oil to light their lamps and lubricate the new machines. The thick fogs and dangerous rocky coasts kept them far out to sea, which protected the Natives, for a time.

In 1812, the Russians established a settlement called Fort Ross north of San Francisco. Decades earlier, the Spanish, later succeeded by the Mexicans, had entered southern California and, with Indian labor, built a chain of missions to fortify their claim to the territory. The farthest north fortification, Mission San Francisco Solano, was built at Sonoma in 1823. In the spring of 1833, the John Work Party, numbering nearly 200 men and women plus packhorses and supplies, trekked north along the coast. They were commissioned by the Hudson's Bay Company to find beaver and other furs for European markets. They shot wildlife to feed their large party and grazed their pack animals as they traveled through the rugged terrain.

In late April, the Work Party camped on the north banks of the Noyo in a rainstorm. Not finding beaver, they continued north. The Yuki, living along the Ten Mile River and vicinity, fled at their approach. The whites had not asked permission to enter Native land. When the whites returned, again without permission, the Natives took action to drive the interlopers out, and clashes between two very different cultures intensified.

Gold-rush hordes invaded all Indian lands. Most found little gold but squatted to claim homesteads. Clashes between incoming whites and the Natives increased. California voted to join the United States in 1850. Federal Indian agents negotiated 18 treaties to establish reservations for 139 tribes, but the US Senate refused to ratify any of them. Two reservations were located in remote parts of Mendocino County in Northern California. In 1856, the Mendocino Indian Reservation was established on the coast; the second reservation was 50 miles inland at Round Valley. In 1857, 1st Lt. H.G. Gibson founded a military post he named Fort Bragg. By 1867, the reservation was abandoned due to scandal and corruption. The remaining Indians were marched on foot to the reservation in Round Valley.

By 1869, the coastal reservation had been returned to public lands, which were surveyed and opened to homesteaders at $1.25 per acre. Former reservation employees preempted the best land, having fenced large areas and occupied empty government buildings. Scottish immigrant A.W. Macpherson, who had built a sawmill at the mouth of the Noyo River in 1858, owned much of the former reservation land near the Noyo River. When he died in 1880, C.R. Johnson, an entrepreneur with ties to Eastern money, purchased the property for a sawmill site, and Fort Bragg Redwood Company began operations in 1885. A wharf at Fort Bragg Landing accommodated small lumber schooners. Chute houses at Noyo Point handled all larger ships. In 1891, after absorbing the Noyo River Lumber Company, the name was changed to the Union Lumber Company. An adjacent mill town grew up and was incorporated in 1889 with C.R. Johnson as the first mayor; it was named Fort Bragg after the former Army post.

One
The World of the First People

This 1863 view is of Big River from the Pomo village of Bul-Dam, located in Northern California. The Pomos and other Native Americans had lived in the area for thousands of years. "Dam" (pronounced "Tom") means "trail." The village, river, and paths over the mountains to the seacoast from inland were all called Bul-Dam. The meaning of Bul is unclear. When white men arrived in the area, all the rivers and forests looked similar to the view above. The Pomo village at the future town of Fort Bragg was called Kah-la-deh-mun, meaning "surrounded by trees." (Photograph by Carleton E. Watkins.)

California's natural bounty supported a Native population of around 310,000 people when the first whites came. Indian trails followed deer trails along ridges from inland to the coast. Indian trails became wagon roads. By 1900, fewer than 20,000 Indians were left in all of the state. (Photograph by W.J. McKie, Union Lumber Company.)

Photographer Edward Sheriff Curtis traveled through Pomo territory between 1900 and 1906, bringing "The Salmon Stream" and other idealized views of the Native people living close to nature back to the public eye. (Photograph by Edward S. Curtis; courtesy of the Library of Congress.)

"The Seed Gatherer" shows a Pomo woman using a "seed beater" and a decorated gathering basket, both woven from local basketry materials. Most Pomo families lived inland and traveled to the coast seasonally to collect seafood, kelp, and salt. They dried or smoked the seafood and kelp for later use. The clamshells were made into "money" for trade. (Photograph by Edward S. Curtis; courtesy of the Library of Congress.)

A "Pomo Man in Dance Costume" has on a headdress made of flicker feathers and a cape of turkey feathers. Dancing was believed necessary to keep the world healthy and in balance. Men's movements were energetic, the women's movements were subtler. Drumming was done with the feet on a length of a hollow oak log. (Photograph by Edward S. Curtis; courtesy of the Library of Congress.)

Pomo shelters on the coast on the Mendocino Indian Reservation were made of bark and brush. After mills began sawing lumber, they included lumber discards. This image was made in 1863. (Photograph by Carleton E. Watkins.)

An 1857 lithograph illustrates how the basket was carried using a tumpline around the forehead as a Pomo woman gathered acorns. (Drawing by Alexander Edouart.)

This 1857 lithograph shows how Pomo men netted fish in the ocean waves. They made hunting and fishing traps from coarsely woven willow branches, which allowed the water to wash through, while trapping the fish as the wave receded. (Drawing by Alexander Edouart.)

Before contact with white people, Pomos constructed shelters from slabs of redwood bark, pried off using elk antlers for wedges. After sawmills were built, they often included lumber discards. This photograph was made in 1902. (Photograph by Samuel A. Barrett.)

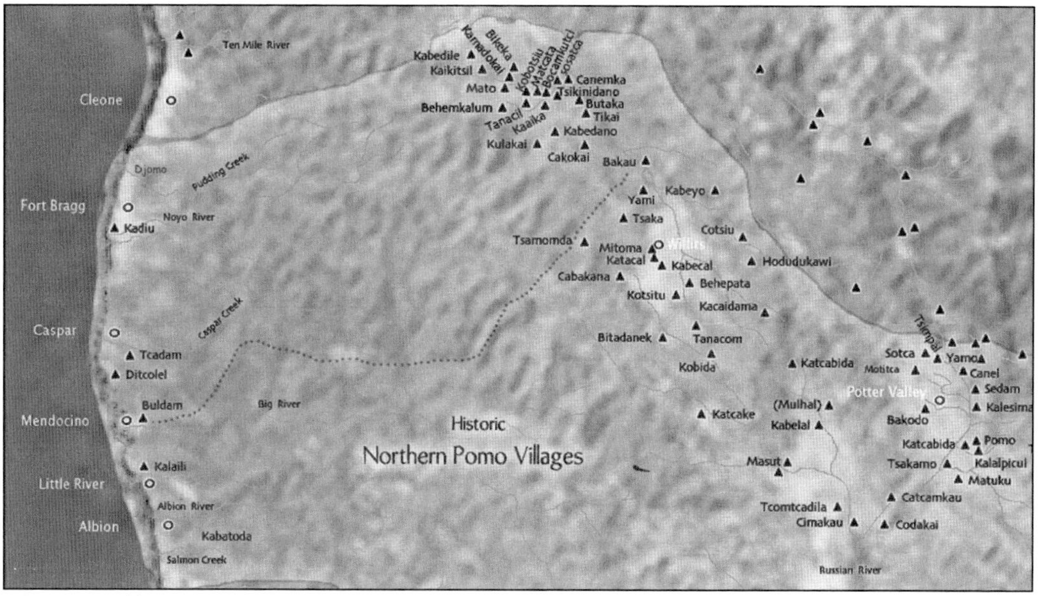

This map of historic Northern Pomo villages and trails was created from information collected by Samuel Barrett and other anthropologists who interviewed Pomos about local historic sites. Site information was overlaid onto a modern topographical map for accuracy. The full-sized color original is on display at the Guest House Museum in Fort Bragg. (Courtesy of Rick Hemmings.)

In 1903, Union Lumber moved the Pomo village at Fort Bragg to an abandoned mill site at Noyo Beach, which, years before, had been part of the Pomo village of Kadiu. The sweat lodge stood near the river mouth. To build a jetty along the river's mouth, the village was again moved in 1929 to the north headlands. (Courtesy of Harriet Rhoades.)

After the Indians were moved to the beach at Noyo, their village site was used as a pasture for horse and sheep and, in the 1930s, as a golf course. (Courtesy of Denise Stenberg.)

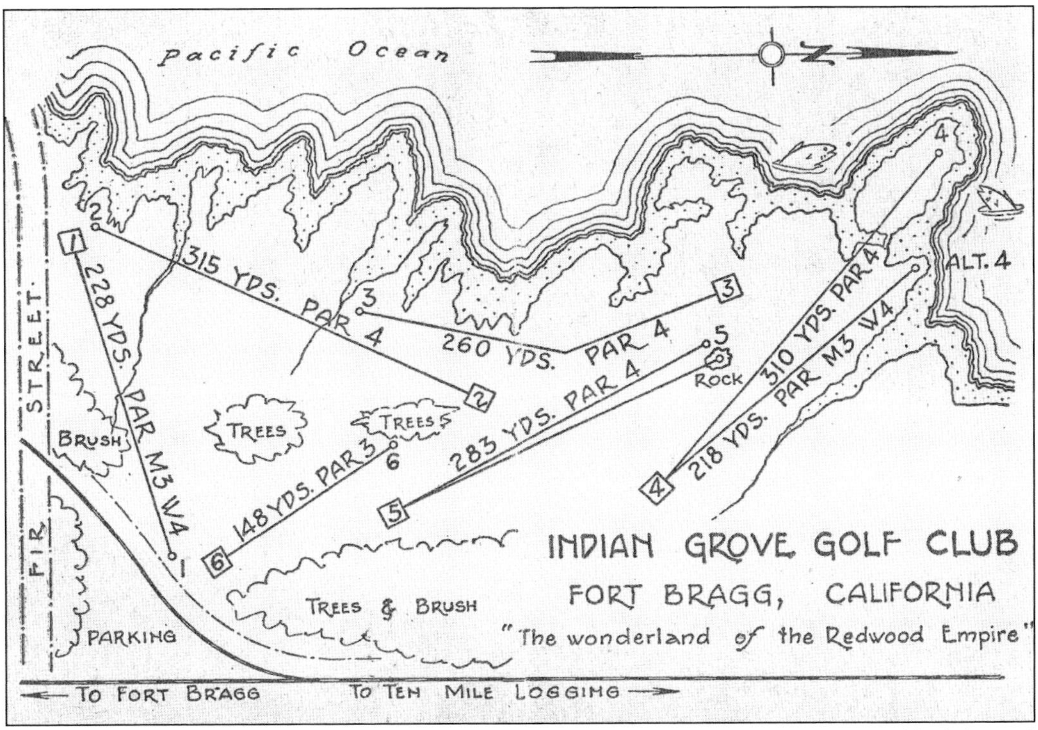

The nine-hole golf course in the former Pomo village area was the Indian Grove Golf Club, used by Union Lumber Company owners and their friends.

"A Madonna of the Redwood Empire" is the title of this photograph. A Pomo baby is laced snugly into a cradle that was made especially for her by a close family member. Traditionally, the cradle was used as a chair once the baby learned to walk.

The Pomos' beautiful, skilled basketry is world renowned. Charmian Cotton Robinson is admiring Lucy Cooper's baby cradle and baskets. They are pictured at Fort Bragg in the summer of 1939.

Two

An Indian Reservation and Army Post

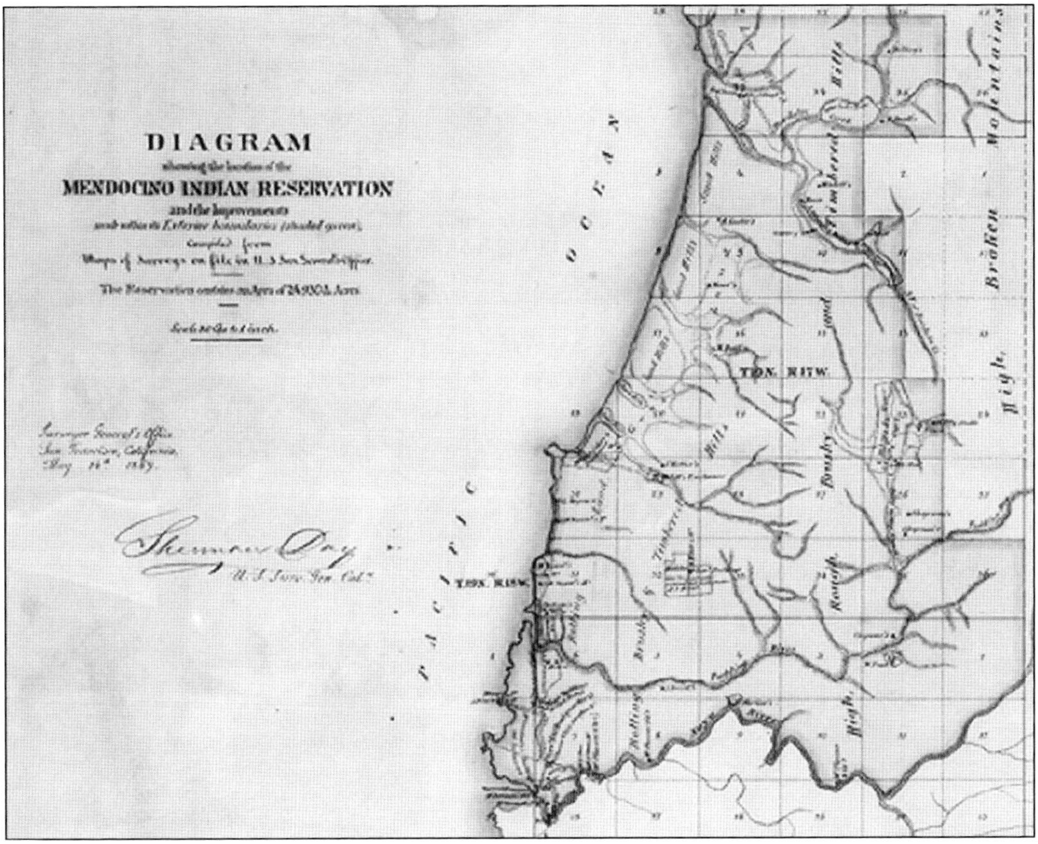

On the coast, the Mendocino Indian Reservation was formalized in 1856; the second was 50 miles inland at Round Valley. The coastal reservation's boundaries included nearly 25,000 acres, extending from the Noyo River on the south to about a mile north of the Ten Mile River, called Bi-dah-toh by the Yukis, east to the foothills of the coastal mountains. Due to scandals caused by corruption of the superintendent of Indian affairs, local authorities, and white settlers, the reservation was abandoned in 1867. These were the boundaries when it was returned to public lands. Reservation employees "preempted" portions of land they wanted and occupied the Army post's buildings. Former reservation land was finally surveyed in 1868–1869 and then opened to homesteaders at $1.25 per acre. (Courtesy of the National Archives, Record Group 49.)

"The buildings of the station stood on a slightly elevated plain, about a mile from the sea, and nearly the same distance from the mouth of Noyo. There were . . . a large storehouse, offices and mess hall, the dwelling of the Agent and some smaller cottages for employees. There was a physician's and an apothecary's accommodation and a number of workshops." (Above, 1863 photograph by C.E. Watkins; left, 1857 drawing by Alexander Edouart.)

While stationed at the Presidio in San Francisco, 1st Lt. Horatio Gates Gibson was ordered to establish an Army post on the Mendocino Indian Reservation to prevent an "Indian War" threatened by white settlers there. In June of 1857 he chose a site about a mile north of the Noyo River for the Post, naming it for a former commanding officer, Capt. Braxton Bragg. Later, both became generals. Gibson, seen in this c. 1860 portrait, stayed in contact with the town into his 90s, sending $5 after the 1906 earthquake to help people in "his town."

This painting of the Fort Bragg Army post parade was made by artist Alexander Edouart during an 1857 expedition recounted in "Reminiscences of Mendocino," *Hutchings California Magazine*, October 1858. Lieutenant Gibson commissioned the painting, which he later donated to the young City of Fort Bragg. A copy of the oil painting is displayed at the Guest House Museum in Fort Bragg.

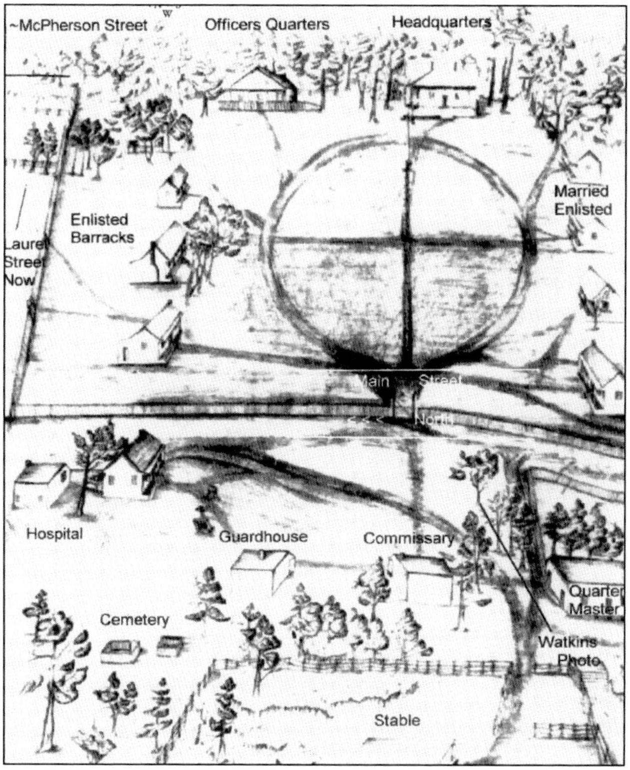

C.E. Watkins's point of view, indicated at left of the Fort Bragg Army post, resulted in the photograph below. One station agent for the Mendocino Reservation lived here; a second Indian station and agent with his assistants lived north of the Ten Mile River; a third, northeast on Bald Hill; and the fourth, south of the Noyo River at Culle Bulle. The original sketch was by Colonel Hull with the labeling added later.

The Army post of Fort Bragg's buildings and parade ground are pictured in 1863. Three soldiers lie in the grass at middle-right. (Photograph by C.E. Watkins.)

This 1857 depiction of the Mendocino Indian Reservation at the Noyo River features the reservation's small fishing boats and Captain Rundle's fishing station. (Drawing by Alexander Edouart.)

The Noyo River Lumber Company Mill is seen in this 1863 view looking west. Alexander Macpherson got permission from Supt. Thomas J. Henley to construct a sawmill in 1858 at the mouth of the Noyo River on reservation land. This and other illegalities caused a scandal that forced the removal of Henley from office. (Photograph by C.E. Watkins.)

This view, looking to the northeast, is of the Noyo River Lumber Company. The reservation's small sailboat is moored at the dock. Workers' cabins line the area north of the sawmill. This 1863 stereograph was made by C.E. Watkins.

Upriver in 1863, a ferry crossed the Noyo, and a settlement grew up around the sawmill. Noyo had the best port between Eureka and San Francisco. There were hotels, stores, saloons, a post office, and dance halls. The trestle carried freshwater in a pipe to the sawmill, crossing beneath the river. (Photograph by C.E. Watkins.)

Here is the ferry crossing before the first bridge was built in 1867. John Byrnes's hotel and barns on the south side of Noyo were enlarged after securing a county franchise to build a toll bridge to replace the ferry. The bridge brought him much more business. (Photograph by M.M. Hazeltine.)

A dietary staple for the coastal Natives, who took only what they needed, was fish. Fish were eaten fresh or smoked or dried in the sun and stored for the winter. However, whites had to learn to appreciate the balance of nature. These sportfishermen display 30-to-40-pound king salmon, common in the 1920s. Word spread, and before long, the elk and grizzlies were gone, and a few years later, the salmon population was in decline.

Before long, in salmon season, fishing boats jammed the Noyo River, as seen here in the 1920s. (Photograph by H.H. Wonacott.)

Times were difficult during World War I. In 1922, nine Finnish fishermen left Noyo for Soviet Karelia. Success of the "workers' revolution" in 1917 attracted idealistic men who wanted to participate in the new "experiment."

The New World offered young people new opportunities. Companies seeking skilled workers advertised in Europe. Popular novels in Finnish and other languages appealed to landless peasants who had little hope for a better future. Most immigrants arrived between 1890 and 1920. Of the woods workers in Fort Bragg and Mendocino County, many were Finnish, Scandinavian, Portuguese, and Italian, with some Germans, Russians, Croatians, Asians, and others. (Courtesy of Noyo Hill House.)

In 1860, the Homestead Act was passed to encourage immigrants to move West and lay claim to the "open land." Natives already living there were pushed off. When they fought back, settlers and the Army killed them. Reservations were established to "keep the peace," but the settlers also desired the reservation lands. Pictured is the Charles Huhtala homestead. (Courtesy of Noyo Hill House.)

Fort Bragg's largest store, owned by the Union Lumber Company, was originally built about 1887. It was rebuilt in 1912 and remodeled in 1920. (Photograph by W.T. Fitch.)

Small independent stores could not compete with the Union Lumber Company until the mid-1920s, when there were independent haulers and year-round roads. This photograph was made around 1912.

Three
REDWOOD "GOLD"

The flood of forty-niners soon sought other ways to make a living. Many claimed homesteads and began farming. Inland, hops, vineyards, and orchards were planted. On the coast, the giant redwood forest attracted lumbermen from the East and Midwest. The huge trees required new tools, methods, and machinery. This picture is from about 1925. (Photograph by H.H. Wonacott.)

In 1883, Charles Russell "C.R." Johnson, who had come West from Michigan with connections to Eastern money, joined owners James Hunter and Calvin Stewart of the sawmill at Ten Mile River. They were hauling lumber by horse-drawn and mule-drawn wagons to ship from Newport, a distance of 10 miles. A better shipping arrangement was needed.

In 1883, mules are seen pulling a small flatcar from the log pond on Mill Creek to the Hunter, Stewart and Johnson sawmill.

A bull team in the Ten Mile mill's woods is hauling logs to a railroad landing in the 1880s. Railroads were built to help access large timber too far from rivers to be transported to a mill by water. Very large redwoods were split with black powder into manageable chunks in order to transport them on small "bob-cars." (Photograph by A.O. Carpenter.)

Here, in about 1884, the *Golden Gate* is loading at an apron chute at Newport. It was the first ship to transfer equipment from Newport south to the new mill site at Fort Bragg Landing. Apron chutes could only accommodate lumber or other items one at a time. Loading ships was a very slow process. (Photograph by Ira C. Perry; courtesy of Kelley House, Mendocino.)

C.R. Johnson bought part of the former Fort Bragg Army post and Mendocino Indian Reservation property, which had deepwater access at Noyo Harbor in addition to a small cove. Starting in 1884, he constructed a wharf and moved the mill machinery by sea. He remodeled a former fort building to live in and named the site Fort Bragg, after the former Army post.

Pictured around 1886, the Johnsons' home at the new mill site was made from remodeled fort buildings. On the porch, C.R. holds his newborn daughter Emily.

Posed on the front steps in 1887 are C.R. Johnson with his parents, Otis and Emily Johnson; his wife, Mary Conness Johnson; and her cousin Edward Wells. Daughter Emily holds her father's hand. Son Otis was also born while they lived in this remodeled fort building at the Fort Bragg mill site. (Courtesy of C.J. Johnson.)

Culle Bulle Station was the southernmost of the four Mendocino Reservation Indian stations. When the reservation (1856–1867) was abandoned, former employees claimed the land and buildings. Only the small house at the right, an original fort-era building, still stands on this property. This postcard is from the 1880s. (Courtesy of Mendocino County Museum.)

Since all travel was by sea, a wharf at Fort Bragg Landing was necessary to bring in all machinery, tools, supplies, and workers to build the new sawmill and to ship wood products out. A steam-powered donkey engine provided the lifting power. Wharf construction began in 1884 and was completed in 1886. It was expanded as production increased.

The SS *Brunswick* tows a sailing ship to the open sea from the wharf at Fort Bragg Landing in 1908. (Photograph by W.T. Fitch.)

The S.C. *Allen* loads lumber at Fort Bragg Landing's wharf around 1910. Only smaller "dog-hole" schooners or sailing ships could access the mill's wharf. (Photograph by W.T. Fitch.)

The Mendocino Lumber Company's yard and wharf in San Francisco handled the Mendocino Lumber Company's production in 1865, as seen here. By 1886, Fort Bragg Redwood Company was delivering its lumber here as well. Before 1905, Union Lumber Company had bought the company.

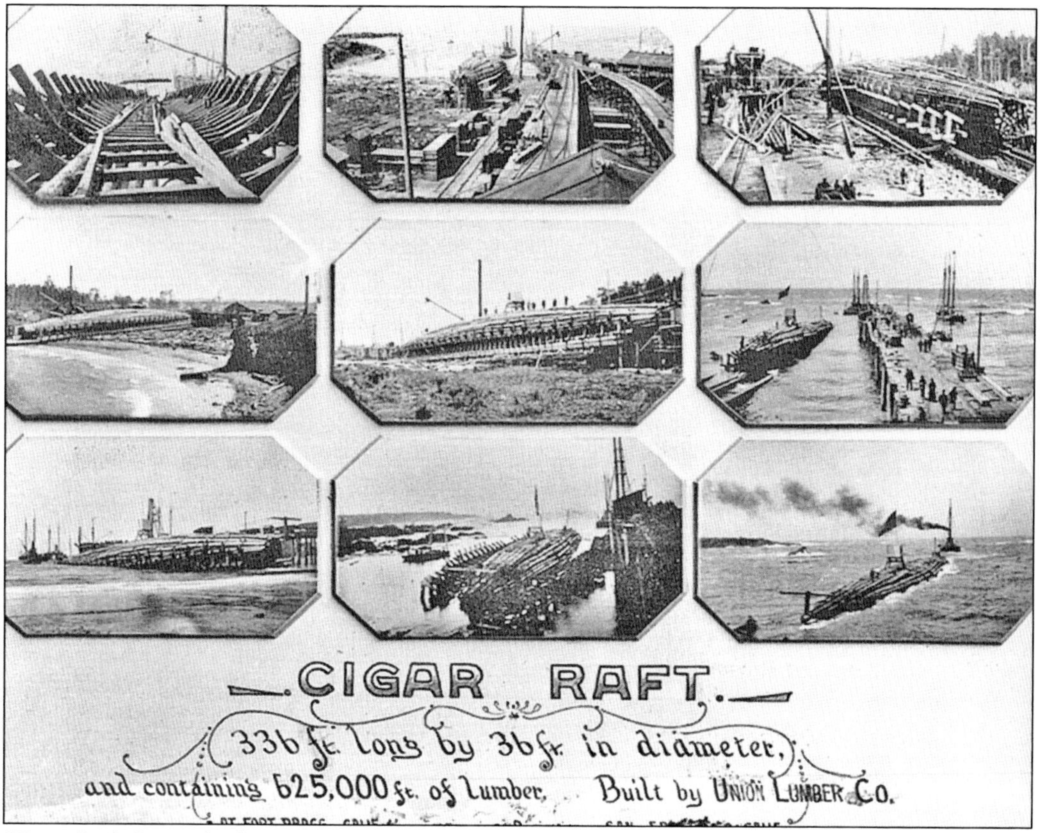

"Cigar Rafts" were built at Fort Bragg Landing by Union Lumber Company. Many attempts were made to tow huge rafts of logs to mills in San Francisco for processing into finished lumber there; however, most log rafts broke up at sea due to wave action. Until this method of transportation was abandoned, nearly all of the logs were lost along with the massive chains binding them together. These photographs were made around 1890. (Photographs by A.O. Carpenter.)

Newsboy, shown above at Union Lumber's wharf about 1890, was Scottish immigrant Robert Dollar's first boat. He started by buying a small mill and wharf at Usal north of Fort Bragg. Although the Usal wharf was destroyed by winter storms and the mill burned, Dollar persevered, founding the worldwide Dollar Shipping Lines.

The *Sea Foam* sank at the Union Lumber Company wharf in 1922. *Sea Foam* transported lumber and passengers between Fort Bragg and San Francisco. The coastal fleet has left many of their bones on the sharp rocks. In this case, the ship was refloated and repaired. (Courtesy of James Ciro.)

Bark was stripped from Tan Oaks, so called for their tannic acid, from which came the term "tanning" of leather. The debarked trees were left to rot in the woods. Here, four mules are seen carrying one cord of bark.

Freight wagons replaced many mules hauling tan bark to load onto ships. In time, trains replaced horses, mules, and wagons.

Here, four men demonstrate railroad tie making around 1900; the man at left is measuring and marking the log; a second man is driving wedges along the lines to split out the ties; a third man is sawing a log section to the right length; the fourth man is smoothing and shaping the ties with a broadax. (Photograph by W.T. Fitch.)

In an undated view of the shipping yards at Noyo Point, tan bark on the train cars and railroad ties and lumber await shipment. This stereograph is from the 1880s.

Fallers pose in an undercut in the 1880s. Double-bit axes and long two-man handsaws, called "misery whips," took between three and five 12-hour days to fall a redwood. Springboards, seen at their feet, provided scaffolding to work above the trees' spreading bottoms and tough roots. (Photograph by W.T. Fitch.)

Pictured in the 1880s, mule teams are hauling pilings on skid roads to load onto train cars at landings. Long, straight pilings were used to construct bridges, wharves, ships' masts, and, later, telephone and electric poles. (Photograph by A.O. Carpenter.)

In the 1880s, 14 bulls were towing a log train near Fort Bragg. Skid roads were made of small logs laid across a cleared dirt track. A water slinger wet down the skid road so that the logs could slide more easily. Bull punchers cursed and used sharp-pointed goad sticks to get the bulls moving. (Photograph by A.O. Carpenter.)

Here, men are building a splash dam. Since logs were floated downriver to the mill, impounded water and winter rainstorms added to the flow to sweep the logs downriver. Booms were constructed along the rivers to corral the logs and prevent them from escaping to the ocean. Note the workmen standing along the dam's top edge. M.M. Hazeltine made this stereograph in 1868.

The Helgate Dam is releasing impounded water to wash the logs downriver. Before trains, river driving was the way all logs were moved from the woods to the local mills. This dam was last used in 1937. The Union Lumber Company bought the mill and remaining timber from the Mendocino Lumber Company in the mid-1930s, during the Great Depression.

Logjams formed in drier years, when many logs did not reach the mill. In exceptionally rainy years, logs could break through the booms constructed to corral them, and a whole year's logging and wages for the loggers would be washed out to sea. This stereograph was published in 1870.

Here, logs are stranded at a boom. The tops of the booms are visible on the left. Booms stopped the logs from continuing down the river into the ocean. Some of the bigger logs were wedged so tightly into the mud and each other that black powder was used to blast them apart. This stereograph was published in 1870.

The logs were combined into rafts, which were towed downriver to the mill by steam-powered barges. All early river driving was done this way. In time, Union Lumber, based in Fort Bragg, bought this operation and other smaller local mills and timberlands. This stereograph is from about 1867.

The SS *Maru*, a steam-powered barge on Big River, towed log rafts, recovered sunken logs from the river bottom, and moved men and material wherever needed.

Pudding Creek became a log pond. A steam train in the distance was bringing more logs to dump into the dammed creek. The Fort Bragg mill needed these logs when heavy rains closed the woods operations, at which time logs were reloaded onto train cars to supply the sawmill. (Photograph by W.T. Fitch.)

As easy timber along the rivers receded and as too much or too little rain made river driving undependable, logging railroads began to replace river driving. The ridge dividing the Glen Bair area from Pudding Creek was cut through by hand. The dirt and rock created the new railroad bed, pictured here around 1905.

To reach new timber, a new railroad was built straight north from Fort Bragg along the coast, going then inland along the Ten Mile River. A steam shovel had to be brought in, as seen here in 1917.

A few years earlier, the railroad had been extended along the Noyo River to connect with the Northwestern Pacific at Willits. Gulches had to be filled and trestles constructed to bridge the winding river. This image is from 1910. (Photograph by W.T. Fitch.)

Tunnel No. 1 for the California Western was built to access timber farther east. The asking price for the intervening property, owned by White & Plummer of the Noyo River Lumber Company, was more than C.R. wanted to pay. Instead, he decided to tunnel through the rocky ridge dividing Pudding Creek from Noyo River.

Johnson hired experienced Chinese tunnel men in 1891. Anti-Asian vigilantes routed the Chinese out of camp in a rainstorm. Sheriff "Doc" Stanley brought them back and arrested the leaders. The tunnel was completed in 1892. Surveyor Markle stands at right with his equipment. (Photograph by Gilfillan.)

Connecting the railroad between the coast and inland was explored as early as 1891 but would not be completed until December 1911. Ironically, the building boom following the 1906 earthquake made it financially feasible. This photograph was made in 1910. (Photograph by W.T. Fitch.)

A wood-burning locomotive is pictured at the wye on the Noyo River around 1905. From left to right are Jim Gordon (far left), Tony Cooney, William Green, Fred Hansen, and Sam Finney. (Photograph by W.T. Fitch.)

Specially geared locomotives were needed to handle the steep terrain and sharp turns. The locomotives, like everything else, were transported on small steamships. Union Lumber Company used the California Western Railroad & Navigation Company, established in 1905.

Locomotive overboard! Not all risky maneuvers were successful. Engine No. 12 was being transferred from a steamship onto the Union Lumber Company's wharf. It dropped through the wharf into the salty Pacific—not recommended for metal machinery—but it was recovered, repaired, and operated successfully.

The California Western had more than 40 railroad bridges and trestles between Fort Bragg and Willits. Two of the "A-frame" bridges, crossing the Noyo River in flood, appear above. The accident pictured below occurred 1.5 miles west of Hayshed Gulch on the Noyo River in 1924. A serious threat to logging train safety was the stability of the loads of logs. Here, a log rolled off a car ahead of the locomotive. The A-frame bridge, already stressed by flooding of the Noyo River, collapsed after being hit by the log. Fortunately, no one died in this accident. The A-frames were replaced with stronger bridges.

The first sawmill at Fort Bragg was built with Ten Mile Lumber Company mill machinery, which was transferred to the new site starting in late 1884. In November 1885, operations began. The mill burned down in 1888 but was immediately rebuilt and enlarged.

Here is the Union Lumber Company's mill around 1900. From the seaward side of the mill looking east, Fort Bragg can be seen in the distance. At left is the fire department's hose-drying tower. Just right of the water tower is the steeple of the Catholic church. The elevated tracks lead to the wharf. H.R. Baum created this hand-tinted photographic postcard.

Five redwood logs, all from the same tree, have been loaded onto flatcars, with one log per car, are seen in 1910 in the rail yards at the sawmill in Fort Bragg. Some logs were too large to fit onto early railcars and were blasted into smaller pieces using black powder. (Photograph by W.T. Fitch.)

This 1901 interior view of the Union Lumber Company sawmill shows an innovative band saw, used to cut huge redwood logs. Band saws replaced circular saws, which wasted a lot of the wood and were too narrow. Circular saws also required logs more than 14 feet in diameter to be blasted apart with black powder.

Fine finishing work was done for Union Lumber at Acme Lumber Company in San Francisco. After a few years, Union Lumber bought this mill, too. Here, a redwood log "float" advertises redwood as a new building material.

West of the sawmill at Union Lumber Company, the elevated track leads to stacks of lumber awaiting shipment about 1900. A lower road leads to the wharf where waiting schooners take on lumber and off-load freight.

Children often brought lunches to relatives at the sawmill, as seen on this rainy day in 1900. Boys often started working in the mill and woods at age 14. Note the lunch pails the children are carrying.

Here are Union Lumber Company's sawmill and log pond at night in October 1960. In 1969, C.R.'s grandson would sell out to Boise-Cascade, and in 1973, Boise-Cascade would sell to Georgia-Pacific. (Photograph by Ed Freitas.)

Shake City, pictured in 1910, was the last woods camp established by Union Lumber along the Noyo River watershed. Big timber was running out after 30 years. Union Lumber looked north to timber along the Ten Mile River watershed. (Photograph by Frederick's Studio.)

Pictured around 1910 is the foreman's quarters at Shake City, Union Lumber's last woods camp on the Noyo River. (Photograph by Frederick's Studio.)

This is the Union Lumber Company's Camp No. 2's dining hall at Ten Mile. Until switching to trucks in 1949, train cars moved portable cabins on to the next campsite. (Photograph by Ed Freitas.)

The Chinese cooks at Camp No. 2 at Ten Mile provided lots of good food for the hardworking woodsmen. Head cook Henry Choy and assistant Kai K. Wong were well liked. Anti-Asian prejudice of the late 19th century faded as neighbors got to know one another. (Photograph by Ed Freitas.)

By 1920, most logs came from Ten Mile. The last logging train crossed the Pudding Creek trestle in 1949. The rails were taken up, and the Haul Road was converted for off-road trucks. (Photograph by W.T. Fitch.)

Today, the remains of the Haul Road have been added to MacKerricher State Park. Since 2005, it is part of the coastal trail between Oregon and Mexico. (Photograph by Ed Freitas.)

After the rails were removed in 1949, huge off-road trucks replaced the trains. This truck is on the Haul Road near the mouth of the Ten Mile River. (Photograph by Ed Freitas.)

The mill, pictured in the 1950s, used more than a million gallons of freshwater a day. Equipment in the mill and woods was constantly modernized to stay competitive in the marketplace. Water jets removed dirt and rocks embedded in the bark, which dulled or broke saw teeth. (Photograph by Ed Freitas.)

In October 1955, sparks from the constantly burning slash fire along the shoreline ignited the log decks. Strong northwest winds had blown sparks into the decks. Fort Bragg's fire chief had repeatedly warned the company of the fire danger. (Photograph by Ed Freitas.)

Open flames were knocked down in about 10.5 hours, but for three days and nights, firefighters came from as far away as Ukiah to join Fort Bragg residents fighting the fire in the log decks. About 10 million board feet of redwood, worth $500,000, were destroyed. To compensate for the loss, Union Lumber bought the holdings of Caspar Lumber Company and proceeded to "log" the old-growth still in Caspar's millpond. (Photograph by Ed Freitas.)

In 1892, Union Lumber had constructed a cottage as a home for the mill manager and for company visitors, overlooking the mill site and town of Fort Bragg. In the 1980s, it housed the company's boutique before being donated to the City of Fort Bragg as the Guest House Museum. (Photograph by Steve Gillette.)

This is an interior view of Otis Johnson's Craftsman-style, all-redwood, "honeymoon" cottage, built for him when he and Marion Marvin married in 1912.

Four

TIMES OF GREAT CHANGE

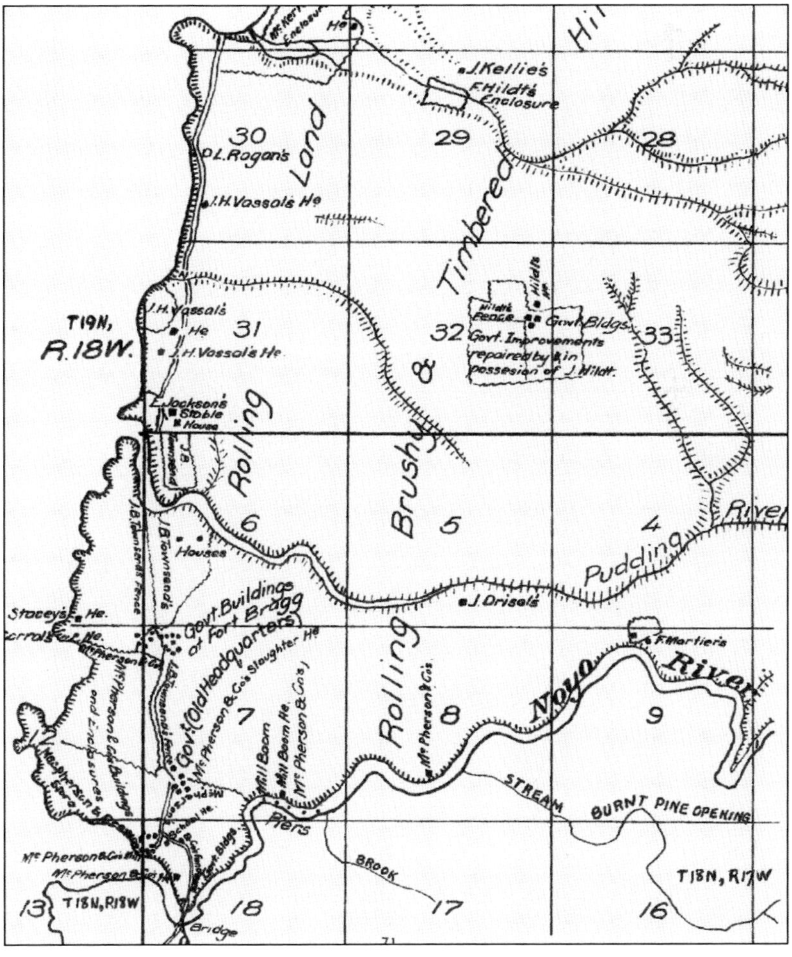

The surveyor's map shows the Fort Bragg vicinity in 1866. In 1867, the reservation was formally abandoned. The area was returned to public lands, and once surveyed, it was opened to homesteaders for purchase at $1.25 per acre. Lumbermen moved in, quickly buying up vast tracts of timber. They often paid men to pose as homesteaders on timberlands they wanted and then bought their land patents. (US Geological Survey.)

An aerial lithograph, printed by the Bucholtz Brothers, shows Fort Bragg in 1891. Fort Bragg incorporated in 1889 with C.R. Johnson as the city's first mayor. The sawmill and wharf are in the central foreground.

John Byrnes's enlarged hotel and barns are shown after the first bridge was built in 1867 across Noyo River. Some 25 years before Fort Bragg was founded, the first businesses and residences were near the sawmill, which had the best deep harbor access for transport and shipping. A.W. Macpherson constructed the sawmill in 1858 on the Mendocino Indian Reservation at the mouth of the Noyo River.

Railroad ties are awaiting shipment at Noyo Harbor. By the 1890s, the Noyo River sawmill belonged to White & Plummer, who were supplying much of the demand for railroad ties to access timber inland. In 1891, Fort Bragg Redwood bought out Noyo River Lumber and became Union Lumber Company.

Seen in 1895 is wood-burning Locomotive No. 3 of Fort Bragg Railroad, hauling logs from Pudding Creek to the sawmill in Fort Bragg 12 miles away.

Tourists and railfans came from near and far to ride the 40 winding miles along the Noyo River, crossing the Coast Ranges between Fort Bragg and Willits, beginning in June 1912. (Courtesy of David Foucheaux.)

Fifty years later, in 1964, the California Western line returned to steam. They purchased and restored a steam locomotive, renumbered as 45, to attract the many railfans who sought out antique railroads as vacation destinations. Steam trains then hauled both lumber and passengers. (Photograph by Tom Moulin.)

Celebrations were held in Willits and Fort Bragg on December 9, 1911. By connecting to the Northwestern Pacific in Willits, Union Lumber guaranteed its preeminence over all other mills in the county. The panic of the 1890s, which the company barely survived financially, was finally overcome by the boom times of rebuilding cities following the 1906 earthquake and fires.

Motor Car No. 80 provided regular passenger service. According to legend, this railbus, joined by Nos. 100, 200, and 300, were dubbed "Skunks," due to the smell of the fuel oil they burned. They delivered mail and groceries to campers and picked up and dropped off fishermen, all in a normal day's run. (Photograph by H.H. Wonacott.)

By 1900, the iron horse had replaced most horseflesh. Behind the well-dressed passengers is the original Willits depot. Fred Goranson, California Western's engineer, stands with his crew at right. (FB–MCHS, Goranson Collection.)

Here we see a well-dressed lady fording a stream. In the countryside, transportation still required real horses.

By the latter 1880s, Fort Bragg's dirt Main Street sported some handsome buildings downtown. The original Hotel McMullen, which was built in 1885 and burned in 1897, was rebuilt to become the Johnson House Hotel, which burned and was rebuilt as the Hotel Kimball, destroyed by fire in 1891. The Hotel Windsor, also three stories, took its place, to be partially burned in 1976. The small structures down the street were mostly saloons, bottling works, and liveries. New immigrants built hotels, stores, and residences on the southwest side of town, where treetops are visible.

This is the Union Lumber Company store in 1897. Fort Bragg Redwood had merged with Noyo River Lumber in 1891, becoming Union Lumber Company. In 1892, a south wing was added to house the Fort Bragg Bank, and in 1895, a north wing was constructed for the new telephone switchboard.

The Union Lumber Company's new store and warehouse, designed by the Reid Brothers of San Francisco, was built in 1912, suffered a fire in 1914, and was remodeled in 1920. The dark building across the street was Red Men's Hall. A service station occupied the corner lot. The Fort Bragg Bank had moved into its own building just north of the company store in 1904.

On Main Street at Alder Street around 1925 was the Grand Hotel with the Grand Service Station on the corner. The next street north is Redwood with Hotel Windsor on the northeast corner. Main Street was first paved in 1923. (Photograph by H.H. Wonacott.)

Fort Bragg's schools included, from left to right, City Grammar (1889), Union High School (1908), and Park Grammar (1895). There was a sharp struggle around building a high school. The company manager fought it all the way to the Supreme Court of California and lost. At issue was taxation of property to support a high school district. H.R. Baum created this hand-tinted postcard.

In the high school's domestic science class, both boys and girls received instruction in cooking and sewing as well as languages, science, history, drama, and music. This 1917 view shows a cooking class.

The *Breath of Ocean*, the Fort Bragg High School class annual, was produced by juniors and seniors with faculty oversight. It contained student photographs, writing, and artwork. The 1909 edition was printed by the *Fort Bragg Advocate*.

Here is a photograph of the 1908 high school track team. Cornelius Vander Starr, wearing the black shirt, excelled in academics and athletics. A hundred years later, his Starr Foundation funded a portion of a new community center, named the C.V. Starr Center in his honor, in Fort Bragg. From left to right are (first row) Fred Kemppe, Edd Aulin, and Willie Hyman; (second row) Joe Dean, Charlie Cavanagh, and Donald Dean; (third row) Clyde Ware and Allen Lesoldin; (fourth row) Cornelius Vander Starr. (Courtesy of Denise Stenberg.)

Fundraising events were staged at community groups' halls, and students, fraternal organizations, churches, and everyone in town participated. The mill and local construction companies donated materials or sold them at cost to help build Fort Bragg's Community Club. (Photograph by H.H. Wonacott.)

In October 1921, Dr. Preston broke ground for the Community Club. By 1922, the building was completed, supported by local subscriptions. Its gymnasium, swimming pool, and meeting and reading rooms were used by the schools and community. (Photograph by H.H. Wonacott.)

In December 1921, the Community Club's cornerstone was laid. Governor Stevens and other dignitaries came for the ceremony as onlookers stood in the rain. (Photograph by H.H. Wonacott.)

In 1930, the Scouts Patrol Conference participants posed in front of the Community Club. (Section of a panorama by H.H. Wonacott.)

All school classes utilized the gymnasium, especially in bad weather. The Community Club's facilities were supported and used by the entire community. (Photograph by H.H. Wonacott.)

This is an interior view of the Community Club's meeting and reading area. The billiards table (at right) was very popular. (Photograph by H.H. Wonacott.)

Here is the swimming pool before it was filled with seawater, which was heated by the mill's boilers. Although salt water killed many pathogens, the iron pipes soon corroded. The switch to freshwater required adding chlorine as a disinfectant. (Photograph by H.H. Wonacott.)

Elementary and high school students learned to swim in the Community Club swimming pool. (Photograph by H.H. Wonacott.)

By the late 1920s into the 1930s, swimming marathons were held at Ten Mile River. Spectators and their cars lined the county bridge and riverbanks. Local students, accustomed to swimming in seawater, enjoyed an advantage. The Finnish Ruuska brothers repeatedly won. Weikko became a swimming teacher. His daughter Sylvia Ruuska won a place on the US Olympic swim team in 1956 and competed in the Summer Olympics in Melbourne, Australia. (Photograph by Everett Racine.)

This is a favorite local racehorse, Mad Anthony, with his owner, trainer, and jockey. An early racetrack was constructed on the north side of the Noyo River.

Pictured is the Blome, Corenson & Landers Greater Show. Traveling carnivals, circuses, speakers, and other entertainers set up during holidays in isolated locales. Local bands, athletes, and theater

During the Great Depression, locals hunted, fished, raised chickens, gardened, and canned, working hard to feed themselves and their families. Here the Ericksons, Mankinens, and Jacobsons of the Finnish collective, Sointula ("Harmony"), some eight miles east of Fort Bragg, together with some friends, neighbors, and two trained hunting dogs, had captured a four-point buck to put food on their tables. Pictured in August 1939, the three women in the group are, from left to right, Bea Erickson, Sylvia Erickson Backlund, and Elma Mankinen. (Photograph by Oscar Erickson.)

groups also traveled to put on entertainment and to participate in judged competitions. This photograph was made between July 1 to 4, 1922. (Section of panorama by H.H. Wonacott.)

Here is the local Improved Order of Red Men's group portrait. The Finnish Kalevala Brotherhood, Odd Fellows, Eagles, Lions, and other fraternal orders, together with local churches, cared for members' and the community's needs long before insurance or Social Security existed.

Here are two views of the Noyo River Tavern. The "Skunk" line opened new territory for "summer resorters" in the 1920s. City folks traveled to the country and camped in large airy tents with lodge conveniences, including a café.

Resorts in the 1920s offered camping close to nature, hiking, fishing, and hunting. Such activities were popular with city folks escaping hot summer weather before air-conditioning.

Townsfolk also camped. The tall redwoods provided shade, quiet time close to nature, relaxation, and time to socialize, while escaping the coast's ocean fogs of summer. This image was made around 1900. (Photograph by Henry R. Baum.)

Seen in the ford around 1900, horses provided the motive power for transportation, whether for work or pleasure, before the advent of the automobile. (Photograph by Henry R. Baum.)

Horse-drawn stagecoaches connected passengers to the iron horses of the California Western at Alpine, a distance of 12 miles, until June of 1912, when regular passenger trains could travel all the way through and back Fort Bragg to Willits. (Panorama by W.T. Fitch.)

Dirt roads meant choking dust in the summer and mud and deep ruts in the winter. In dry weather, horse teams pulled road scrapers to build or smooth roadbeds.

The second Ten Mile River bridge was built in 1914 by the Sallinen brothers and crew, local Finns. The Ten Mile River was so named because it was ten miles north of Noyo River, the main local port. This was the last bridge on the Coast Road built for public access. Residents petitioned Mendocino County for improvements to assure safe travel for residents, freight, and the US mail.

In 1924, a section of the second county bridge across the Noyo River collapsed. Traffic had increased, and loads were heavier. After Homer Barton's Shell Oil truck broke through a section into the river, a third stronger bridge was built in 1927. (Photograph by H.H. Wonacott.)

Pictured in 1924 is one of the automobile dealers in Fort Bragg. With the coming of the automobile, livery stables turned into garages and car dealerships. In Fort Bragg, one could buy Fords, Reos, Studebakers, Nashes, Willys, and more. (Photograph by H.H. Wonacott.)

Here is a member of the fleet of the local Coast Line Stages. By the 1940s and 1950s, transportation between towns, coast, and inland was provided by "auto stages." For travel out of the county, Greyhound buses were the chief carriers. Trains carried mostly freight and lumber. (Photograph by H.H. Wonacott.)

When nothing useful was left on a car, Conway's Garage towed the remains to the city dump, as seen here around 1920. (Photograph by H.H. Wonacott.)

Over time, the location of the city's dump migrated north, involving three different sites along the oceanfront. This picture is form the 1920s. One-time trash is now considered "treasures." Tourists come from all over to visit Glass Beach; the ocean has reworked the dumps' many-colored rounded shards of glass from bottles. (Photograph by H.H. Wonacott.)

Tall, shady redwood forests were cleared. People thought there were so many huge trees that they could never all be cut down. As the forests disappeared, so did the wildlife living in them. (Photograph by Norman R. Coulter.)

The Mathison Ranch, pictured in 1911, was a typical homestead. Lumber companies sold the logged-off land, called "stump ranches," to homesteaders. The huge redwood stumps resprouted from the roots. In the hilly terrain, farming required endless labor.

Pushing back redwood forests, homesteaders built houses, put up fences, planted gardens and orchards, and raised hay for livestock. Continuous logging and destruction of the redwood's new growth gradually opened farmland. Today, only about three percent of the original redwood forest remains, mostly in parks. These postcard were published around 1910. (Photograph by W.N. Wood.)

Apple orchards were cultivated on former forestland. The lumber companies advertised farmland for sale after clearing the trees. This photographic postcard was published around 1910. (Photograph by W.N. Wood.)

Five

From Tribulations to Celebrations

On April 18, 1906, an earthquake on the San Andreas Fault, which passes just offshore, destroyed much of downtown Fort Bragg, demolishing most brick buildings and chimneys, as fire consumed the wooden structures. (Photograph by W.T. Fitch.)

Deep gulches required numerous trestles for railroads. The top photograph shows a 1,000-foot-long trestle on the Caspar Southfork & Eastern Railroad over Jug Handle Creek, about a mile south of the Noyo River, before the 1906 earthquake.

Here is the same trestle after the earthquake on April 18, 1906. Estimates of the magnitude range between 7.9 and 8.3. Ferries had to be placed back into service to cross local rivers. Structures needed to access timber for the sawmills were immediately rebuilt.

The damage to the Fort Bragg sawmill and yards was extensive. One side continued reduced operations, but it was three months before full production could be resumed. (Photograph by W.T. Fitch.)

Here, at Franklin and Laurel Streets, is some of the 1906 earthquake's damage. Fire destroyed what the quake did not. All the town's water lines were broken. Luckily, the steam schooner *National City* was at the wharf and pumped water from the ocean, saving much of the downtown. (Photograph by W.T. Fitch.)

The Bank of Fort Bragg is pictured before and after the 1906 earthquake. Of about six brick buildings, only two survived, although damaged. Chimneys were thrown down. Next to the bank building constructed in 1904, the company's Guest House lost five all of the brick chimneys for its seven fireplaces. (Below, photograph by W.T. Fitch.)

Homeless families, by necessity, had to camp out. The mill made lumber available and collected payment after the men went back to work. By 1908, the town was mostly rebuilt. (Photograph by W.T. Fitch.)

In 1908, Fort Bragg's downtown merchants created a joint fund and constructed water towers and stations for fire protection. The view is looking northeast on Redwood Avenue. These buildings were hotels, boardinghouses, and saloons.

Fred Kemppe's beer truck is on the way to supply the town of Albion around 1910. With so many single workingmen, the number of saloons ballooned. Fort Bragg had about 40 drinking places in town, far outnumbering the churches.

The Standard Bottling Company, pictured around 1940, prepared and bottled extracts for sodas. Bulk beers, like Lucky Lager and Acme, were also bottled in Fort Bragg.

Prior to Prohibition, the Christian Women's Temperance Union worked tirelessly to outlaw alcohol due to its ruinous effects on families. A formal portrait showed these beer drinkers' position on the issue. (Photograph by W.T. Fitch.)

Illegal stills appeared out in the woods during Prohibition. Federal "revenuers" put some out of business, but local authorities often accepted a cut of the business in return for looking the other way. Many locals became rumrunners. Liquor was big money when "Baby Face" Nelson was in Fort Bragg.

"The Island of Joy" featured a shack on an island just offshore from the sawmill. Connected by two swinging bridges, it was reputed to be a saloon and brothel. After a young salesman fell off one bridge in broad daylight and died, the town mothers demanded the establishment be shut down. In 1921, the cables connecting the bridges to the shore were mysteriously dynamited.

Passage of the 18th Amendment in 1919 brought Prohibition to Fort Bragg. Fueled by preachers' fiery sermons, feminine outrage at the damage to families caused by alcoholism was empowered by, at long last, winning the right to vote, sweeping the Volstead Act into law. On February 7, 1923, a river of bootleg liquor ran in the gutters in front of the Fort Bragg Fire Department on Main Street. Former saloons, which had long outnumbered the churches in town, were converted into garages, shops, and stores.

To get around illegalities concerning alcohol, some outfits advertised shows featuring a "blind pig," a metaphor, in rural humor, for bootleg whiskey. There were disappearing bars, hidden rooms, midnight deliveries, and increasing corruption.

Unable to agree on how to amend the law's glaring problems, together with the economic crisis of the Great Depression, the government instituted new taxation and regulations for liquor. Joyful celebrations greeted the repeal of Prohibition in 1933. (Photograph by H.H. Wonacott.)

In 1895, Finns belonging to Lännentoivo, which means "hope of the West," built a temperance society hall and boardinghouse for single men to combat the abuse of alcohol. After passage of the 18th Amendment in 1919, they sold the hall to the Kalevala Brotherhood and Sisterhood, a group who cared for sick and injured members and buried those who died. Now, it is the Lions hall.

Toveri Tupa, "Comrades' Hall," was built by volunteer labor in 1914. It was a lively cultural center, hosting dances, musical programs, plays, as well as meetings and public events. Community and church halls were rented for large gatherings. Now, it is the Eagles hall.

The Fort Bragg Co-op Store is pictured around 1940. In 1923, local Finns established the first consumers' and producers' co-operative in the state of California. Meeting minutes were in Finnish into the 1940s. They trucked in tons of feed and supplies from Petaluma and shipped back hundreds of crates of eggs. Petaluma hatcheries delivered chicks via US mail. Co-op members bought on credit, settling up when they got paid. The membership held annual picnics at Camp No. 20. After a potluck, youngsters played baseball and swam while the older folks played bingo and visited.

Here is a Finnish play cast on stage in 1911. Classical and modern Finnish dramas were regularly staged in Fort Bragg. They performed at festivals from the Bay Area to Eureka and Astoria. Prizewinning Finnish choruses toured with their professional directors. (Photograph by O.L. Dowe.)

During the Great Depression, a Verigreen pea packing plant was constructed on the north end of Franklin Street. There, peas were shelled and packed in ice. In the 1930s, over 100 boxcar loads of fresh green peas, strawberries, and huckleberries were shipped each year to markets as far away as New York. (Photograph by H.H. Wonacott.)

In the early 1930s, workers of Verigreen Fruit and Vegetable Company of San Diego went on strike and won a few cents more per hamper (25 pounds) of perishable peas. (Photograph by H.H. Wonacott.)

In 1934, during the Great Depression, two camps of unemployed young men worked in Mendocino County. The Civilian Conservation Corps (CCC) camp was at Russian Gulch on the coast. They learned skills, built bridges and schools, and created public facilities, such as the lodge, cabins, and trails at the Mendocino Woodlands and Russian Gulch State Park; these structures, plus other local park facilities, are all still in use. (Courtesy of the National Archives.)

In Fort Bragg, the CCC boys built a new high school and auditorium. The auditorium was named for J.S. Cotton, a longtime teacher and principal. He and his wife moved their house so that the auditorium could be constructed next to the high school. The first class graduated in 1939. (Photograph by H.H. Wonacott.)

Pictured in 1937 is the construction and dedication of the new high school and auditorium. The importance of this project to Fort Bragg was indisputable. Everyone pitched in to move it forward and celebrated its completion. The building complex, dedicated in 1937, was restored in 2005. (Photographic collage by H.H. Wonacott.)

Bea and Oscar Erickson (left) began work on founding a senior center in 1973. Elizabeth "Liz" Irwin (right) was the director of the senior center from 1974 to 1982. The center was named in her honor after she died. (Both, author's collection.)

Part of the school complex was rededicated as the Bea Erickson Senior Center in 1983. Bea Erickson, coastal director of North Coast Opportunities, secured a section that did not meet new seismic safety standards for schools for a senior center. The center, a statewide model, has since been privatized due to state and county budget cuts. (Author's collection.)

In 1913, the Mendocino County Products Fair and Festival, a countywide fair with parades and events, boosted local fruits, vegetables, livestock, games, and competitions, which became an annual countywide fair. Above, the parade heads south on Main Street in Fort Bragg.

It took countless hours to prepare the decorated autos and floats for the 1913 celebrations. Decorations covering parade entries were made with locally grown flowers, ferns, and greenery.

"Paul Bunyan," also known as six-foot, eight-inch, Charlie Buck, greets Angelo Rossi, mayor of San Francisco. In 1939, still in the grips of the Great Depression, Fort Bragg established a unique Labor Day celebration, called Paul Bunyan Days, showing off the skills of the lumberjacks. The Golden Gate Bridge had opened in May 1937. "Paul" invited city folks to drive up north and join the fun. By the turn of the century, with old-growth timber gone, mills closed, and fish stocks depleted, Northern California's legal economy would shift from lumber and fishing to tourism.

Union Lumber Company's parade entry is pictured at the first Paul Bunyan Days, hosted September 1–4, 1939. From left to right are Frank Fernandez, as Chief Noyo; C.R. Johnson; Otis Johnson; Russell Johnson; and Charlie Buck, as the first Paul Bunyan. (Photograph by Gabriel Moulin Studios.)

The Fort Bragg Bakery created a train of bread loaves with roll wheels and breadstick logs for Paul Bunyan Days. (Photograph by H.H. Wonacott.)

Pictured are promoters of Paul Bunyan Days in 1939. Women dressed in colorful gingham and sunbonnets, and men grew beards and donned plaid shirts, boots, and jeans. They pose in front of the company's Guest House. (Photograph by Gabriel Moulin Studios.)

This is the State Theater during the first Paul Bunyan Days. Businesses decorated their exteriors with redwood bark provided by the Union Lumber Company. (Photograph by H.H. Wonacott.)

Here is the 1954 high pole climbing event. Showcased at Paul Bunyan Days were various specialized skills. One event demonstrated climbing and topping trees to create spar trees, used to hoist and move logs for loading onto trains or trucks. Danny Sailor, British Columbia champion high pole climber, danced a jig atop a spar pole. (Photograph by Ed Freitas.)

Out in the logging woods, Ole Granvall, Union Lumber Company faller, is seen demonstrating tree topping at the third annual Junior Logging Conference, held May 1–4, 1955. (Photograph by Fred Landenberger, RRCC.)

Chainsaw event contestants were judged on the speed and technique with which they cut through a sizeable log. The winner of this event in 1951 was Ralph Todd. (Photograph by Ed Freitas.)

"Bull o' the Woods" was a new event in 1967 that put boxing gloves on two lumberjacks on top of a fallen log. In this contest, Russ Camelleri (right) bested Dale Miller (left). Standard events featured skills needed in the logging woods, including hand ax chopping, ax throwing at a target, chainsawing, and high pole climbing. (Photograph by Ed Freitas.)

This photograph shows "Westward Ho," the first-prize float of 1957. Floats were sponsored by local organizations and competed for a variety of prizes. (Photograph by Ed Freitas.)

Paul Bunyan in 1968 was Chet Shandel, standing six feet, four inches. The clown was Chris McKinnon, and Uncle Sam was Dewey Main. All three men attended the adult and kiddie events. (Photograph by Ed Freitas.)

The author's father, Oscar Erickson, was a skilled logger for 30 years. He would often voice doubts about the long-range effects of logging methods. "The woods are so quiet now," he would say. "When I was young they were alive with the sounds of birds and wildlife." And, "What are young people going to do for work here after all of the trees are cut down?" (Photograph by author.)

This image is from the "Redwood Summer" of 1990. Protesting corporations' cutting and running, hundreds of idealistic young people traveled to Fort Bragg. Street theater, live music, and speakers invited loggers fearing the loss of their livelihood to listen and talk. The outcome was peaceful but recalled earlier times of protest. (Photograph by author.)

This lumber train was picketed in Santa Rosa in 1946. The Redwood Region had serious labor-management disputes in 1897 and 1903–1907. On entry into World War II, wages were frozen, but prices had already risen sharply. After the war, a wave of strikes swept the country as workers sought parity between wages and prices. (*Press Democrat* photograph, author's collection.)

"Paul Bunyan was a union man. Why not you?" During the 1946–1948 strike in Fort Bragg, the union sponsored Paul Bunyan Days when the company declined to do so. In 1947, the company again sponsored Paul Bunyan Days, but on the Fourth of July instead of Labor Day. The strike ended in February 1948. (Photograph by W. Hornzee; author's collection.)

This is the "Last Log Sawn. Official Portrait." The last log sawn at the Fort Bragg mill was a media event held August 8, 2002. Local media included the *Advocate*, *Beacon*, *Santa Rosa Press Democrat*, and the author of this book. The crew was expected to help celebrate closing the mill, despite the loss of their jobs. Employees dropped from a high in the 1980s of over 1,200 down to 3 guards and night watchmen. (Photograph by author.)

Pictured is "the Sawmill Crew's 'Gift'." Before the official image above was made, the crew gave a handmade redwood sign to the mill manager, which read, "Ron . . . This log should not be our last to cut . . . This log should be shoved up your butt." (Photograph by author.)

The other basis of the local economy was fishing. John Mattila, a Finnish fisherman at Noyo, posed with a 65-pound king salmon around 1910. It was not unusual for commercial boats to bring in huge quantities of gigantic fish, which would be hard to believe today. Fishing boats grew in numbers and size, while logging silted in gravel streambeds salmon needed to reproduce.

Many Italian, Portuguese, and Finnish people made a comfortable living by salmon fishing and working at fish packing plants. Their success attracted more fishermen and boats. Over time, the once bountiful resource was depleted. (Photograph by H.H. Wonacott.)

By 1936, the Noyo River needed dredging to deepen it. Logging upriver exposed steep hillsides to erosion during winter rains, which then washed downstream. (Photograph by H.H. Wonacott.)

Problem rocks, which had sunk various boats entering during low tides or heavy swells, were blasted out by the Army Corps of Engineers at the mouth of the Noyo River. (Photograph by Addie Ries.)

Here is the second Noyo River bridge before a section collapsed in October 1924. A third bridge replaced it in 1927, just upriver, but larger trucks and loads soon made that one inadequate as well. By 1947, the US War Department had declared the third bridge a menace to navigation.

The fourth Noyo Bridge was completed in 1948. A steel bridge high above the river, it was unaffected by high water, and larger boats could pass below. A marina was built upriver in 1967. With logging trucks now using public roads, stronger bridges with easier access were required. (Photograph by CalTrans; courtesy of Jim and Barbara Hurst.)

Six

Local Culture and Rural Humor

Many Civil War veterans came West and claimed homesteads. They farmed cutover land or worked in the sawmills or the woods. They hunted and fished to supplement their income. North-South conflicts came West with the immigrants to Mendocino County. There were brawls, fisticuffs, and shoot-outs.

William Bennett, a bachelor and electrician at the mill, created a family by carving them out of redwood. The family included a father, a mother, and five daughters, all life-sized. He dressed them all in tailor-made clothing. They often accompanied him on the front porch on warm evenings. When Bennett's health began to fail, he "cremated" them in his backyard and died soon after. "Fort Bragg's Wood Family" story appeared in the *San Francisco Examiner* on May 29, 1911. (Photograph by H.H. Wonacott.)

The grand marshal and his staff are at the 1900 Fourth of July parade. Many Civil War veterans continued to wear their uniforms and occupied law enforcement positions. They also organized celebrations such as Decoration Day, now called Memorial Day. (Photograph by W.T. Fitch.)

Here, people are racing barrels on Main Street around 1900. Many celebrations were informal and spontaneous. Horseraces were also run on Main Street in Fort Bragg before it was paved.

Family picnics on Sundays in good weather were common. People visited, fished, swam, and rested. People seem dressed up in old-time photographs, but most had only one set of good clothes in addition to their work clothes. (Courtesy of Noyo Hill House, Ross collection.)

Four Finnish families celebrate the 10th anniversary in 1912 of the founding of Sointula, "Harmony," a commune on 636 hilly acres eight miles east of Fort Bragg. Included in this photograph are the Mankinens, Ericksons, Andersons, and Jacobsons. Sointula lasted 55 years. This map of Sointula was made by retired cartographer Clarence Erickson. He is second from the left in the first row in the photograph above. The men worked in the woods and made railroad ties to earn money while the women tended the home front. On Wednesdays and Saturdays, they bathed as family groups in a communal sauna. Tools, a blacksmith shop, horse barn, team and wagon, large orchard, and potato and hay fields were all shared communally. (Both author's collection.)

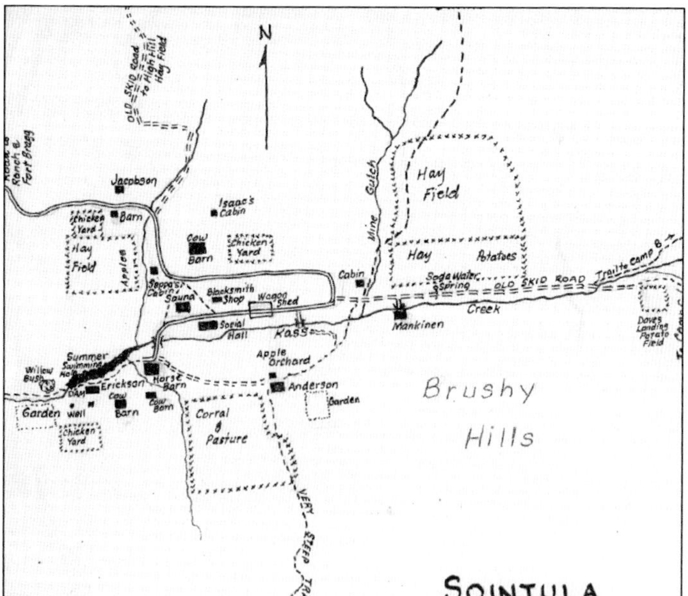

Here is a c. 1920 Finnish funeral leaving Kalevala Hall on the way to a burial ground. The local chapter of the Kalevala Sisterhood organized in 1895 to care for sick and injured members and to bury those who died. The Kalevala Brotherhood joined them 10 years later. Community service groups met such needs long before Social Security began in the 1930s during the Great Depression.

Community picnics were held in Fort Bragg's City Park on the northeast edge of town from 1891 to 1922, when Union Lumber logged it. The Fort Bragg School District built a new school there in 1928. Park Grammar School was built here in 1895. (Photograph by H.H. Wonacott.)

This 1924 postcard is titled "A Mendocino County Minnow." Humans employ humor to help them cope, often making light of unsettling aspects of life. As an example of rural humor, this photographic postcard records the deceased whale's statistics as "70 feet long" and "45 feet around at the waist line."

Not all deer hunting involves guns or bows and arrows. At times, humor is in the unexpected. A boy with a camera pursued this doe across the beach at Cleone and up onto wave-washed rocks. The boy got the shot, and no one got hurt. However, both parties got wet.

Here is a c. 1930 freight truck at the California Western Railway Depot in Fort Bragg. (Photograph by H.H. Wonacott.)

Although it looks like a scene from the 1930s during the Great Depression, the license plate says 1947. Located behind the trailer is a "No Parking–Taxi Stand" sign. But Fort Bragg did not have any taxi stands. (Photograph by H.H. Wonacott.)

Pictured around 1905, these young men were able to earn a few dollars by hunting and trapping. (Courtesy of Alan Nelson.)

Henry R. Baum, Fort Bragg's pharmacist, posed with orphaned bear cubs for tourists. Note his thick leather gloves and protective clothing.

Here is a "tight-wire act across Main Street." Many traveling entertainers and shows visited small towns during good weather. This view is from a Fourth of July before the 1906 earthquake. (Courtesy of Harry Shafsky.)

Pictured around 1915 is wash day at Caspar Lumber Company's Camp No. 1. Adolph Backlund washes clothes on the porch of the bathhouse, as Matti Jylka plays a button accordion. Caspar had out-maneuvered Union Lumber for timberland along the Noyo River. (Author's collection.)

Independent and Hollywood films are still made here. A silent film, *The Signal Tower*, was filmed among the coastal redwoods along the California Western Railroad in 1923 and premiered in Fort Bragg at the Liberty Theater on Franklin Street.

The challenge for Northern California nearly 200 years later is the necessity to find a balance between environmental and human needs. Together with a historical consciousness, important insights may help to create a new future. This image is from the 1880s.

Here is the "Fort Bragg, 1857–1957, Historical Landmark No. 61." On the centennial of the founding of the Army post of Fort Bragg, a bronze plaque mounted on a pink limestone boulder from inland Mendocino County was dedicated. Dignitaries present were Gen. Robert N. Young, US 6th Army; Evelyn Cotton, the widow of Joel S. Cotton, Fort Bragg's longtime teacher and principal; and Sgt. Gilbert Friberg, Army Reserves and Union Lumber Company employee. (Photograph by Ed Freitas.)

A fifth bridge now spans the Noyo River. Bridge No. 4 was completed in 1948 and replaced in 2005. Modern construction is engineered for earthquakes up to magnitude 8 on the Richter scale. The San Andreas Fault is only four miles offshore. (Photograph by author.)

This 1952 aerial view is of the Union Lumber Company mill site and Fort Bragg. Shipping by sea ended in 1933, after the longshoremen's union attempted to unionize the sailors, and Union Lumber Company switched to trucking. The last of the wharf (a single tall timber still visible in this image) was destroyed by a storm in 1962. The sawmill closed in September 2002. Decontamination of the more than 400-acre industrial site is ongoing. The Noyo Marine Science Research Center and a coastal trail along the shoreline are in the plans. Discussions continue on how to best use the site. Townsfolk at long last will soon gain access to their town's shoreline. (Photograph by Clyde Sunderlund.)